Amazon, Paypal, eBay

A road map and history

In 1995, Amazon.com sold its first book, which shipped from Jeff Bezos' garage in Seattle. In 2006, Amazon.com sells a lot more than books and has sites serving seven countries, with 21 fulfillment centers around the globe totaling more than 9 million square feet of warehouse space.

The story is an e-commerce dream, and Jeff Bezos was Time magazine's Person of the Year in 1999. The innovation and business savvy that sustains Amazon.com is legendary and, at times, controversial: The company owns dozens of patents on e-commerce processes that some argue should remain in the public domain. In this article, we'll find out what Amazon does, what makes it different from other e-commerce Web sites and how its technology infrastructure supports its multi-pronged approach to online sales.

Amazon.com Basics

Amazon.com sells lots and lots of stuff. The direct Amazon-to-buyer sales approach is really no different from what happens at most other large, online retailers except for its range of products. You can find beauty supplies, clothing, jewelry, gourmet food, sporting goods, pet supplies, books, CDs, DVDs, computers, furniture, toys, garden supplies, bedding and almost anything else you might want to buy. What makes Amazon a giant is in the details. Besides its tremendous product range, Amazon makes every possible attempt to customize the buyer experience.

When you arrive at the homepage, you'll find not only special offers and featured products, but if you've been to Amazon.com before, you'll also find some recommendations just for you. Amazon knows you by name and tries to be your personal shopper.

The embedded marketing techniques that Amazon employs to personalize your experience are probably the best example of the company's overall approach to sales: Know your customer very, very well. **Customer tracking** is an Amazon stronghold. If you let the Web site stick a cookie on your hard drive, you'll find yourself on the receiving end of all sorts of useful features that make your shopping experience pretty cool, like recommendations based on past purchases and lists of reviews and guides written by users who purchased the products you're looking at.

The other main feature that puts Amazon.com on another level is the **multi-leveled e-commerce** strategy it employs. Amazon.com lets almost anyone sell almost anything using its platform. You can find straight sales of merchandise sold directly by Amazon, like the books it sold back in the mid-'90s out of Jeff Bezos' garage -- only now they're shipped from a very big warehouse. Since 2000, you can also find goods listed by third-party sellers -- individuals, small companies and retailers like Target and Toys 'R Us. You can find used goods, refurbished goods and auctions. You could say that Amazon is simply the ultimate hub for selling merchandise on the Web, except that the company has recently added a more extroverted angle to its strategy.

In addition to the affiliate program that lets anybody post Amazon links earn a commission on click-through sales, there's now a program that lets those affiliates (Amazon calls them "associates") build entire Web sites based on Amazon's platform. They can literally create mini Amazon Web sites if they want to, building on Amazon's huge database of products and applications for their own purposes. As long as any purchases go through Amazon, you can build a site called Amazonish.com, pull products directly from Amazon's servers, write your own guides and recommendations and earn a cut of any sales. Amazon has become a software developer's playground.

Before we dig deeper into Amazon's e-commerce methods, let's take a quick look at the technology infrastructure that makes the whole thing possible.

Amazon has four software development centers worldwide. These units are constantly creating new features for Amazon.com and developing the technology to support them.

Amazon Technology

The massive technology core that keeps Amazon running is entirely Linux-based. As of 2005, Amazon has the world's three largest Linux databases, with a total capacity of 7.8 terabytes (TB), 18.5 TB and 24.7 TB respectively [ref]. The central Amazon data warehouse is made up of 28 Hewlett Packard servers, with four CPUs per node, running Oracle 9i database software.

The data warehouse is roughly divided into three functions: query, historical data and ETL (extract, transform, and load -- a primary database function that pulls data from one source and integrates it into another). The query servers (24.7 TB capacity) contain 15 TB of raw data in 2005; the click history servers (18.5 TB capacity) hold 14 TB of raw data; and the ETL cluster (7.8 TB capacity) contains 5 TB of raw data. Amazon's technology architecture handles millions of back-end operations every day as well as queries from more than half a million third-party sellers. According to a report released by Oracle after it helped migrate Amazon's data warehouse to Linux in 2003 and 2004, the central task process looks something like this:

In the 2003 holiday season, Amazon processed a top-end 1 million shipments and 20 million inventory updates in one day. Amazon's sales volume means that hundreds of thousands of people send their credit card numbers to Amazon's servers every day, and security is a major concern. In addition to automatically encrypting credit card numbers during the checkout process, Amazon lets users choose to encrypt every piece of information they enter, like their name, address and gender.

Amazon employs the Netscape Secure Commerce Server using the SSL (secure socket layer) protocol (see How Encryption Works to learn about SSL). It stores all credit card numbers in a separate database that's not Internet-accessible, cutting off that possible entry point for hackers. Customers who are particularly cautious can choose to enter only a partial credit card number over the Internet and then provide the rest by phone once the online order is submitted. Aside from the usual security concerns regarding online credit-card purchases, Amazon suffers from the same phishing problem that has plagued eBay and PayPal, so watch out for fake e-mails asking for your Amazon.com account information. Check out Anti-Phishing Working Group: Amazon.com for details on how to recognize a fake.

Now let's get back to the business of selling stuff. Amazon's approach to e-commerce is one that leaves no stone unturned.

AMAZON PATENTS

Amazon has tried to patent nearly every aspect of its e-commerce architecture, drawing more than a little controversy for the affiliate program patent it won back in 2000. Reportedly, other e-commerce sites were already using affiliate programs that looked a lot like the one Amazon developed and patented. Here are just a few of Amazon's dozens of patents:

Internet-based customer referral system, U.S. Patent 6,029,141, February 22, 2000

Content personalization based on actions performed during a current browsing session, U.S. Patent 6,853,982, February 8, 2005

Method and system for integrating transaction mechanisms over multiple internet sites, U.S. Patent 6,882,981, April 19, 2005

Use of product viewing histories of users to identify related products, U.S. Patent 6,912,505, June 28, 2005

Amazon E-commerce

Amazon.com has always sold goods out of its own warehouses. It started as a bookseller, pure and simple, and over the last decade has branched out into additional product areas and the third-party sales that now represent a good chunk of its revenue (some estimates put it at 25 percent).

Both retailers and individual sellers utilize the Amazon.com platform to sell goods. **Large retailers** like Nordstrom, Land's End and Target use Amazon.com to sell their products in addition to selling them through their own Web sites. The sales go through Amazon.com and end up at Nordstrom.com, Land's End.com or Target.com for processing and order fulfillment. Amazon essentially leases space to these retailers, who use Amazon.com as a supplemental outlet for their online sales.

Small sellers of used and new goods go to **Amazon Marketplace**, **Amazon zShops** or **Amazon Auctions**. At Marketplace, sellers offer goods at a fixed price, and at Auctions they sell their stuff to the highest bidder. Amazon zShops features only used goods at fixed prices. If an item listed on zShops, Marketplace or Auctions is also sold on the main Amazon.com, it appears in a box beside the Amazon.com item so buyers can see if someone else is selling the product for less in one of the other sales channels.

The level of integration that occurs on Amazon is a programming feat that few (if any) online sales sites can match.

Another sales channel called**Amazon Advantage** is a place where people can sell new books, music and movies directly from the Amazon warehouse instead of from their home or store. Sellers ship a number of units to Amazon, and Amazon handles the entire sales transaction from start to finish. In all of these programs, Amazon gets a cut of each sale (usually about 10 percent to 15 percent) and sometimes charges additional listing or subscription fees; in the case of Amazon Advantage, the company takes a **55 percent commission** on each sale. The Advantage channel is something like a consignment setup, a sales avenue for people who create their own music CDs or have self-published a book and are simply looking for a way to get it out there.

One of the latest additions to Amazon's repertoire is a subsidiary company called **Amazon Services**. Through Amazon Services, Amazon sells its sales platform, providing complete Amazon e-commerce packages to companies looking to establish or revamp their e-commerce business. Amazon sets up complete Web sites and technology backbones for other e-commerce companies using Amazon software and technology. Target, for instance, in addition to having a store on Amazon.com, also uses Amazon Services to build and manage its own e-commerce site, Target.com.

But selling goods isn't the only way to make money with Amazon.com. The Web site's affiliate program is one of the most famous on the Web. Through Amazon's **Associate Program**, anyone with a Web site can post a link to Amazon.com and earn some money. The link can display a single product chosen by the associate, or it can list several "best seller" products in a particular genre, in which case Amazon updates the list automatically at preset intervals. The associate gets a cut of any sale made directly through that link. The cut ranges from 4 percent to 7.5 percent depending on which fee structure the associate signs up for (see Amazon Associates for complete program details). The associate can also take advantage of**Amazon Web Services**, which is the program that lets people use Amazon's utilities for their own purposes. The Amazon Web Services API (application programming interface) lets developers access the Amazon technology infrastructure to build their own applications for their own Web sites. All product sales generated by those Web sites have to go through Amazon.com, and the associate gets a small commission on each sale.

Check out Amazon Web Services to learn more about what you can do with Amazon's e-commerce platform.
In the next section, we'll take a look at how all of these programs and channels come together to create a sales and marketing powerhouse.

Amazon Tools, Marketing and Community

The goal is pretty straightforward: "To be Earth's most customer-centric company where people can find and discover anything they want to buy online." The implementation is complex, massive and dynamic. Amazon's marketing structure is a lesson in cost-efficiency and brilliant self-promotion. Amazon's associates link to Amazon products in order to add value to their own Web sites, sending people to Amazon to make their purchases. It costs Amazon practically nothing. Some associates create mini-

Amazons -- satellite sites that do new things with Amazon data and send people to the mothership when they're ready to buy. Amazon Light, built and maintained by software developer Alan Taylor, is one of those satellite sites.

The level of **customer tracking** at Amazon.com is another best-of-breed system. Using the data it collects on every registered user during every visit to the Web site, Amazon points users to products they might actually be glad to discover -- and buy. Amazon recommends products that are:

- similar to what you're currently searching for (on-the-fly recommendations that use up tons of processing power)
- related to what you've searched for or clicked on at any time in the past
- purchased by other people who've searched for what you're searching for or have bought what you've bought

You can even customize the recommendations by giving Amazon more information about yourself and your interests and rating the products you've already purchased.

A recent development in customer tracking actually collects information on people who may have never visited Amazon.com. Amazon's **gift-giving recommendations** collect data on the stuff you buy for other people. For instance, if you buy a toy train set in December and ship it to your nephew, Amazon knows you give gifts to a boy aged four to 10 who lives in Ohio and likes trains. Might your nephew enjoy the latest addition to that train series? Might he also have an interest in RC cars? Amazon will give you all sorts of ideas about what to get your nephew when the next holiday season rolls around.

This type of information gathering has generated a fair amount of controversy. Some say Amazon gathers too much information for comfort, and the Electronic Privacy Information Center reports that in 2000, Amazon started sharing its customer data with its partners and subsidiaries. The concern has increased with the tracking of "gift-giving habits," because the gift-giving information Amazon collects could be about minors, which is against the law, and because the gift receivers don't even know that their name, age, gender, location and interests may be stored in Amazon's database of customer information.

Despite concerns about Big Brother Amazon, tons of people love the personalized experience Amazon offers. It's not just sales offers -- there's a **community** on Amazon.com that's based on people providing even more information about themselves to other Amazon users. People write their own reviews, recommendations, "So You'd Like To..." guides and "Listmania" lists based on Amazon's product offerings and share them with all of Amazon.com. One Listmania list, "The Top 25 Weirdest Items You Can Purchase Through Amazon!" by Sheila Chilcote-Collins of Van Wert, Ohio, includes a jar of S.E.P. (Stop Eating Poop) that should make your dog stop eating its own feces; bird feed in the form of live caterpillars shipped to your doorstep; and a book entitled "Owl Puke" that comes complete with a genuine pellet of regurgitated owl meal. You can make any sort of list you want, and any Amazon member can view it and rate it. (Click here to view the Top 100 Listmania lists.)

Beyond e-commerce and its trappings, some of the more recent Amazon endeavors have the company branching out into new realms. Amazon's **Mechanical Turk** project seeks to combine community, technology and compensation. Using the Mechanical Turk system, software and Web developers can post tasks they need help with, usually tasks related to things computers can't do but humans can, like quickly caption a set of photos. Anyone can post a task, and the person who completes it gets a small amount of money in return. Amazon gets a commission on each completed transaction. In a much more visible trek into the unknown, Amazon has funded the **A9 search engine**. It has full search capabilities, mapping functions, a toolbar with pop-up blocking and an easily accessible personal search history. A9 also provides a "Diary" where you can makes notes to yourself about specific Web pages and lists of recommended links for you to check out based on your previous searches. In keeping with Amazon's omnipresent marketing techniques, you can sign up to get an Amazon.com discount for using A9 on a regular basis, and when you type in a search term, you'll see a display of Amazon book results related to that term.

From a "Where's Amazon going?" point of view, perhaps the most notable project is the previously mentioned Amazon Services subsidiary. **Amazon Services** is building complete e-commerce solutions for companies that are potential Amazon competitors, leaving open the possibility that Amazon will ultimately head in the direction of technology service over retail sales.

THE GOLD BOX AND TIMELINE: A TON OF STORES

There's probably a little "Gold Box" icon at the top of the Amazon.com homepage every time you visit. This box holds special treats for you: Time-sensitive discounts. Once you click on the Gold Box and view an offer, you have to complete the transaction (if you want it) in a specified time period. After that time period, the offer disappears.

- 1994: Amazon.com is incorporated.
- 1995: It sells its first book.
- 1996: It launches its affiliate program ("Associates Program").
- 1997: It goes public.
- 1998: It buys the Internet Movie Database (IMDb) and opens two new Amazon stores: Music and DVD/Video.
- 1999: It launches Amazon Auctions and zShops and opens six new stores: Consumer Electronics, Toys & Games, Home Improvement, Software, Video Games and Gift Ideas.
- 2000: It launches Amazon France, Amazon Japan and Amazon Marketplace and opens two new stores: Kitchen and Camera & Photo.
- 2001: It introduces the "Look Inside the Book" function and teams up with Target stores.
- 2002: It launches Amazon Canada and Amazon Web Services and opens two new stores: Office Products and Apparel & Accessories.
- 2003: It launches Amazon Services and A9.com subsidiaries and opens three news stores: Sports & Outdoor, Gourmet Food and Health & Personal Care.
- 2004: It buys Joyo.com (which becomes Amazon China) and opens one new store: Beauty.
- 2005: It buys BookSurge LLC

In 2004, a South Florida woman listed a partially eaten grilled cheese sandwich on eBay. The sandwich sold to the highest bidder for $28,000. She believed, and showed in the auction's photos, that the sandwich had the image of the Virgin Mary in one of its slices of bread.

EBay is a global phenomenon -- the world's largest garage sale, online shopping center, car dealer and auction site with 147 million registered users in 30 countries as of March 2005. You can find everything from encyclopedias to olives to snow boots to stereos to airplanes for sale. And if you stumble on it before the eBay overseers do, you might even find a human kidney or a virtual date.

In this ebook, we'll find out how you can buy and sell items on eBay, examine how the bidding process works, look at ways you can protect yourself from auction fraud and take a look at the business and technology of the largest auction site in the world.

eBay Basics

EBay is, first and foremost, an online auction site. You can browse through categories like Antiques, Boats, Clothing & Accessories, Computers & Networking, Jewelry & Watches and Video Games. When you see something you like, you click on the auction title and view the details, including pictures, descriptions, payment options and shipping information. If you have a pretty good idea of what you're looking for, you can search for it using simple keywords, such as "Apple iPod," or using more advanced search criteria that helps narrow the results, such as keywords to exclude, item location, price range and accepted payment methods.

If you place a bid on an item, you enter a contractual agreement to buy it if you win the auction. All auctions have minimum starting bids, and some have a reserve price -- a secret minimum amount the seller is willing to accept for the item. If the bidding doesn't reach the reserve price, the seller doesn't have to part with the item. In addition to auctions, you can find tons of fixed-price items on eBay that make shopping there just like shopping at any other online marketplace. You see what you like, you buy it, you pay for it and you wait for it to arrive at your door. There are also auction listings that give you the option to "Buy it Now" for a price that's typically higher than the auction's start price. If you choose to buy the item for the "Buy it Now" price instead of bidding on it, the auction ends instantly and the item is yours.

You can pay for an item on eBay using a variety of methods, including money order, cashier's check, cash, personal check and electronic payment services like PayPal and BidPay. It's up to each seller to decide which payment methods he'll accept. PayPal is the easiest way to buy something on eBay, because eBay owns PayPal. The PayPal payment process is already built into any auction listing on eBay.

Just as you can buy almost anything on eBay, you can sell almost anything, too. Using a simple listing process, you can put all of the junk in your basement up for sale to the highest bidder. Lots of people sell their old laptop once they've upgraded, the clothing their kids have grown out of or the brand new couch they bought on final sale without realizing it wouldn't fit in their den. Some people even make a business of eBay by opening their own "eBay store." When you sell an item on eBay, you pay listing fees and turn over a percentage of the final sale price to eBay.

Once you register (for free) with eBay, you can access all of your eBay buying and selling activities in a single location called "My eBay."

EBay is a massive operation with something like 4.8 million new listings per day. Before we learn more about how to buy and sell on eBay, let's find out how eBay manages this level of activity

eBay Infrastructure

A series of service disruptions in 1999 caused real problems for eBay's business. Over the course of three days, overloaded servers intermittently shut down, meaning users couldn't check auctions, place bids or complete transactions during that period. Buyers, sellers and eBay were very unhappy, and a complete restructuring of eBay's technological architecture followed.

In 1999, eBay was one massive database server and a few separate systems running the search function. In 2005, eBay is about **200 database servers** and **20 search servers**.

The architecture is a type of **grid computing** that allows for both error correction and growth. With the exception of the search function, everything about eBay can actually run on approximately 50 servers -- Web servers, application servers and data-storage systems. Each server has between six and 12 microprocessors. These 50 or so servers run separately, but they talk to each other, so everybody knows if there is a problem somewhere. EBay can simply add servers to the grid as the need arises.

While the majority of the site can run on 50 servers, eBay has four times that. The 200 servers are housed in sets of 50 in four locations, all in the United States. When you're using eBay, you may be talking to any one of those locations at any time -- they all store the same data. If one of the systems crashes, there are three others to pick up the slack.

When you're on the eBay Web site and you click on a listing for a Persian rug, your computer talks to Web servers, which talk to application servers, which pull data from storage servers so you can find out what the latest bid price is and how much time is left in the auction. eBay has **local partners** in many countries who deliver eBay's static data to cut down on download time, and there are **monitoring systems** in 45 cities around the world that constantly scan for problems in the network.

This infrastructure lets millions of people search for, buy and sell items simultaneously. On the user end, it all works seamlessly. Let's try it out.

Using eBay: Browsing for Items

The best way to learn how to use eBay is to dive right in. What do you feel like looking for today? A surround-sound system? A mink stole? HowStuffWorks could use a Homer Simpson Pez dispenser. Let's look for one.

There are two ways to go about finding a Homer Simpson Pez dispenser. We can browse, or we can search. Let's start by browsing -- it's the slower, more round-about method, but it's a good way to get a feel for eBay's category system. The most popular categories are listed right on the eBay homepage, on the left side.

Pez dispensers are typically considered collector items, so the Collectibles category is a good place to start browsing. If we click on the Collectibles link on the homepage, we end up at a page listing all of the Collectibles subcategories.

At the very bottom of the page, there's actually a subcategory called Pez, Keychains, Promo Glasses, and within that subcategory is another subcategory called Pez.

That seems like a good fit. Clicking on "Pez" brings us to an auction-level page

- There are 3,355 listings in the Pez category.
- The listings are currently sorted by time, with the newest auctions first.
- We can search within Pez listings.

Since we're looking specifically for a Homer Simpson Pez dispenser, "Homer Simpson" is a good term to use to narrow the results. If we enter "Homer Simpson" in the search box directly above the listing, it's only going to search the Pez subcategory, not all of eBay (although you can search all of eBay using a dropdown menu in the category field). Here's what comes up:

Thirteen items isn't bad, but we might be able to find more. When you enter a search term and there are fewer results than you'd like, the first thing to do is go back up to the search field and check the box for "Search title **and**description." The first search we did checked only the auction *titles* for the term "Homer Simpson." Searching only titles is a good way to narrow your results if you know exactly what you're looking for and what most people call it -- for example, if you're looking for a GPS receiver, it's a pretty safe bet that anyone selling one would put "GPS" in the title. On the other hand, someone selling a Homer Simpson Pez dispenser might not put "Homer Simpson" in the title -- she might put "Simpsons" or only "Homer." So now we're going to search entire auction descriptions, which typically returns more results:

We now have 23 listings to look through. But there is a much faster way to get to the place we've ended up at. If you're just looking for a bargain on some type of collectible, browsing is the way to go; but if you're looking for something specific, the eBay search function is the quickest way to it.

Using eBay: Searching for Items

At the top of the eBay homepage, there's a search box where we can enter what we're looking for.

When you do a simple search, the auction results page also tells you which categories your results are in. You'll notice that there are matches for Homer Simpson Pez dispensers in other places besides the Pez category. So when we search both titles and descriptions, we end up with 25 results -- more than we did when we were browsing.

There's a listing about halfway down the page for a full set of Simpsons Pez dispensers, including Homer, with a starting price of just 99 cents. That seems like a good deal.

The **starting price** is low, the **shipping price** is reasonable, and the seller has 99.6% **positive feedback**. Always check the shipping price, as some sellers mislead buyers by selling the item for cheap and then making up the difference by severely overcharging for shipping, and always check the seller feedback. The feedback is how you know if you can trust the seller (and your feedback is how the seller knows he can trust you). We'll talk more about feedback in the next section, but for now, we just need to know that 99.6% positive feedback is a good sign.

Since we're interested in this auction, we'll click on "**Watch this item in My eBay**" (top right of the auction page) so we can get back to it easily. Now it's in our watch list:

In the next section, we'll bid on this item

Using eBay: Buying Items

To look for an item, you don't need to register -- you can browse, search and watch items (up to 10) as a guest. You can't bid or buy as a guest, though. So the next step is to register with eBay here. It's quick and free.

Now we can place a bid on the set of Simpsons Pez dispensers. If we click on the link in our watch list, we end up back at the auction page. There are four main sections to any auction page:

- **Title/Overview** - This is where you see the basic information, like auction title, price, shipping price, seller information and how many bids have been placed so far.

   Description - This is where the seller provides details about the item.

   Shipping, payment and return policy - This is where you can find full shipping information, any details the seller wants a bidder to know about making payment (including which methods are accepted) and what the seller's return policy is.

- **Bidding** - This is where you place a bid on the item.

   eBay's bidding process works like this: You enter the maximum amount you are willing to pay for the item, and eBay bids incrementally on your behalf until the bidding reaches the maximum amount you entered. So if we decide we are willing to pay $2.00 for this set of Pez dispensers, we enter $2.00 in the bid slot.

   When we click "Place bid," the next screen is a confirmation screen where we can see the bid price and commit to it.

   The top portion of the page with the blue background is for our eyes only -- no one else can see what our maximum bid is. Why is the current price $0.99 and not $2.00? It's because when you're the first bidder, no matter what you enter as your maximum price, your first bid is always the starting price. If someone bids against us, eBay will bid on our behalf up to $2.00 in $0.05 increments (low-price auctions use very small increments, while high price auctions use larger increments). So if another user comes along and enters $1.25 as his maximum, eBay will bid $1.31 on our behalf, and we'll still be winning. But if another user places a maximum bid of $2.01, we've been outbid (and eBay will send us an e-mail to this effect in case we're not watching the auction). At this point, if we still want these Pez dispensers, we have to enter a new maximum bid.

This is where eBay's bidding process doesn't work exactly like it's supposed to -- and starts to get exciting. If every bidder truly entered the maximum he was willing to pay, auctions would end with little fanfare. The person who entered the highest maximum bid would quietly win. But humans being human, the actual maximum amount they're willing to pay is usually "a tiny bit more than what everyone who's bidding against me is willing to pay." If we still want our Pez dispensers, we'll enter a new maximum bid of, say, $3.00; and as long as the other bidder's maximum amount is less than $3.00, we'll be winning the auction again. Our coup might be temporary, though, because if the other bidder wants these Pez dispensers as much as we do, he's going to bid again until he outbids our maximum. And now we have a bidding war.

Bidding wars are a rush -- and they're sometimes very expensive. If this war continues for the three days until the auction ends, we could end up paying a hundred bucks for these Pez dispensers. It happens. The adrenaline takes over and people start bidding to win -- not necessarily to win a few Pez dispensers, just to WIN. For this reason, most of the bidding happens in the last two minutes of an auction. People wait to place a bid until an auction is about to close -- this way, they can catch other bidders off guard, and hopefully no one will get the chance to outbid them. The last 10 seconds of a bidding war often becomes a battle of bandwidth. Someone using a dial-up connection will never be able to place a winning bid in 10 seconds. Someone using a cable modem can place a winning bid in two seconds.

There is at least one reason why someone would place a bid very early in the auction: to remove a "Buy it Now" option. Remember that when an auction item also has a "Buy it Now" option, if someone decides to "Buy it Now" the auction is over. But the opposite is also true: As soon as someone bids on the item, the "Buy it Now" option disappears. If someone comes across an item she wants but she's not willing to pay the "Buy it Now" price, she'll enter the minimum starting bid just so another user doesn't come along and buy it out from under her.

Feedback

When talking about eBay or any other online auction site, one of the most common questions is "How can I trust the person I'm buying from?" The answer is "feedback." Buyers leave feedback for sellers and sellers leave feedback for buyers whenever they complete a transaction. Feedback can be positive, neutral or negative, and your feedback score is listed beside your username whenever you're involved in an eBay transaction. If you buy an item and never receive it, and the seller doesn't answer your e-mail regarding the lost item, you leave negative feedback. If you sell an item and the winning bidder never pays, you leave negative feedback. If everything goes well, you leave positive feedback. When you're involved in a transaction with someone who has 99.9 percent positive feedback, you can be confident you're not going to get swindled. To learn more, visit the eBay Feedback Forum.

Using eBay: Paying for Items

eBay Resources

- Buyer Resources
- Searching Overview
- eBay Glossary
- All About My eBay
  If we win our Simpsons Pez dispensers, the next step is to pay for the item. The seller in this listing accepts two forms of payment: PayPal electronic payment or money order/cashier's check. Overall, there are typically four methods of payment you can use on eBay:
- Cash
- Personal check
- Paper money order or cashier's check
- Electronic payment

Cash is simple but dangerous, because you have no recourse if it gets lost in the mail, and sending it by registered mail is just going to cost you more money. Personal checks are safer to send in the mail. The downside to paying by check is that once the check arrives, the seller usually waits for it to clear the bank before shipping your item, so it'll probably take you an extra couple of weeks to receive it. With money orders and cashier's checks, the wait time is shorter because there's nothing to clear. Electronic payment is the fastest method -- practically instantaneous. Using sites likes PayPal, BidPay and WesternUnion.com, you can draw money from your bank account or credit card or purchase an electronic money order and send the payment to your seller over the Internet. The downside to e-payments is the risk factor involved in any online transfer of financial data.

Once we complete payment, the seller will ship it to us. The auction states the shipping method as "Standard Flat Rate Shipping Service," which doesn't tell us much, so if we want to know more we'll have to ask the seller. We can do this using the "Ask seller a question" link in the Seller Information box at the top of the auction listing.

Once we receive the item, our next step is to leave feedback. If the seller has met all of her obligations (If the auction stated a shipping timeframe, did the item arrive accordingly? Does the item match the seller's description?), then our feedback should be positive. If we are not satisfied that the seller met the standards for positive feedback, the next move is contact her to try to resolve the issue. Always let a seller try to fix the situation before leaving negative feedback. Most of the time, all it takes is a simple e-mail exchange to solve a problem, and you can't retract negative feedback once you submit it.

eBay Etiquette: Buyer Do's and Don'ts

Do:

- leave feedback for every transaction
- pay within the seller's preferred timeframe
- read the entire listing before asking questions

Don't:

- leave negative feedback before contacting the seller
- leave rude feedback

So far, we've searched for, bid on and paid for an item. Our next step is to sell one.

Outcome: We Got Cocky
Three days later, we were still the only ones bidding on these Pez dispensers, and the author let her guard down. She left eBay and started working on her next article. But it turns out there was competition out there waiting to strike. In the last minute of the auction, three additional bidders turned up, and our set of Simpsons Pez dispensers sold to the highest bidder for $7.50.

Using eBay: What Can I Sell?

You can sell almost anything on eBay -- almost, but not quite. You can't sell illegal items, like illicit drugs, or government-controlled products like liquor, tobacco, guns or prescription drugs. You can't sell lock-picking tools or surveillance equipment like wiretaps or hidden cameras. You can't sell human body parts or remains, like your extra kidney (that's been tried) or your dead uncle's foot, and you can't sell something that doesn't exist in some concrete form -- for instance, you can't sell your soul to the highest bidder. An eBay user named David Finn tried that and got shot down. Just for a glimpse into the complex nature of running a site like eBay, here's an excerpt from the letter Finn received from an eBay representative regarding the decision to pull the plug on his auction:

If the soul does not exist, eBay could not allow the auctioning of the soul because there would be nothing to sell. However if the soul does exist, then in accordance with eBay's policy on human parts and remains we would not allow the auctioning of human souls. The soul would be considered human remains, although it is not specifically stated on the policy page...

For a complete list of no-no's, see What items may not be sold on eBay?. If your item is not listed anywhere in that section, it's probably okay to sell. The author has a refurbished Samsung Yepp MP3 player that she bought on eBay a couple of years ago and never uses. That's definitely OK to sell. In the next section, we'll list this MP3 player on eBay.

Spelling Counts

When writing titles and descriptions, watch your spelling. If we misspell "MP3" as "MP#" by holding down the shift key for too long, the only people who will find our auction are the ones specifically searching for misspellings. People who find these items can get them for super-cheap because no one's there to bid against them. There are Web sites and programs whose sole purpose is to find misspelled auctions on eBay. There's a spell-check button on the "Describe Your Item" page.

Using eBay: Selling Items

We are going to try to sell a refurbished Samsung Yepp MP3 player on eBay. To sell something on eBay, you don't need much -- a few descriptive details is about all it takes. And if your item is in tangible form, it's good to have a picture of it. If we click the "Sell" button at the top of the homepage, we arrive at the first step in the listing process:

We don't have an eBay Store, so we're not going to be selling at a fixed price. And we're not advertising real estate. So we're going to choose "Online Auction." The next step is to choose the category we want our item in. MP3 players definitely belong in the consumer electronics category.

At the bottom of this page, we can choose to list our item in a second category for an additional fee, but Consumer Electronics is the obvious place for buyers to look for an MP3 player, so we'll just stick with that. On the next page, we'll choose "MP3 Players" as our subcategory, "Samsung" as the brand and "Yepp" as the model.

Now it's time to describe the MP3 player we're selling.

The field for the freestyle item description is at the bottom of the page. You don't need to know HTML unless you want to do something fancy with your description (see How Web Pages Work to learn HTML). If your description will look fine as a block of text, you don't need any HTML tags at all. If you want any font changes or spaces between paragraphs, you can use this simple HTML template, which includes a header setup and a few paragraph tags:

AUCTION TITLE

ITEM DESCRIPTION

ADDITIONAL DETAILS

This is what we're going to paste into the description box:

Samsung Yepp 64 MB MP3 Digital Audio Player REFURB

Up for auction is a refurbished Samsung Yepp model YP-30S MP3 player with 64 MB onboard memory. It's also a digital voice recorder. It measures about 2.5 inches tall, 1.75 inches wide and just over 0.5 inches deep. I bought it on eBay a couple of years ago but didn't end up using it much. On the outside, the player is immaculate, and as far I know it works. You can definitely load and listen to music and navigate through your MP3 files. Aside from that, I'm not sure because I never read the manual or tested its various functions.

Along with the player, you'll receive the user manual, installation CD, USB cable (not shown in picture) and carrying case with belt clip.

Next, we'll set a starting price, decide if we want to provide a "Buy it Now" option and set the auction duration. A little research tells us that a brand new Samsung Yepp YP-30S is selling for about $90, and a refurbished one is selling for about $40. Since we can't say for sure that every function on this player works, we'll start the bidding low -- at $9.99. This is a good idea for several reasons:

- It provides incentive for someone to buy this MP3 player even though the seller is somewhat uncertain as to its condition.
- It lets people consider buying it just for parts.
- It cuts down on the listing fee we'll be paying to eBay, because part of the listing fee is based on the starting price.

Setting a reserve price, which is the lowest price at which you're willing to sell your item, costs extra, and it really only makes sense to set one when you're selling a high-value item. In that case, starting the bidding at the lowest price you're willing to accept would mean a very high listing fee, so you might start the bidding low but pay a small fee to set a reserve. We've chosen not to set a "Buy it Now" price because auctions are fun, and we've gone with the standard, 7-day auction that will start as soon as we submit our listing. Next, we're going to scroll down a bit and add a picture.

We're using **eBay Basic Picture Services** because we only have one picture to load, and the first picture is free. All we have to do is click "Browse," locate the picture on our hard drive and double-click the file. If you have only a few pictures and you're not selling 50 items a week, it makes sense to use eBay's system. Otherwise, you might want to look into the cost-effectiveness of going with your own **image-hosting service**.

The rest of that page is filled with additional features that you can purchase for a fee, including bold-face type for your title, a fancy frame for your listing and a spot in the "Featured Items" box that begins any list of search results. We're going to pass up those extras in order to keep our listing price down.

On the next page, we choose our payment methods and set our shipping fee. We're going to make this a PayPal-only auction to keep it simple (and because the author already has a PayPal account), and we'll estimate our shipping cost so buyers know up front what they'll be paying if they win. We could also wait and send the winning bidder the shipping cost once we know his zip code, or we could set up a shipping calculator that allows the buyer to enter his zip code and find out the exact shipping charge. A seller can ship using any carrier, including the U.S. Postal Service, UPS and FedEx, or the seller can let the buyer choose the shipping method once the auction ends.

At the bottom of this page, we establish our return policy and provide any additional payment instructions if we have them:

The final step is to review our listing details on the next page and make sure everything is correct. If not, we can makes changes and review it again. The bottom of this page shows our total listing fee:

eBay charges an **insertion fee** of $0.35 for starting prices between $1.00 and $9.99. We didn't purchase any additional features, so that's all it costs us to list this item. When someone buys the MP3 player, we'll also pay eBay a **final-value fee**. If it sells for $25.00 or less, the fee is 5.25 percent of the final sale price. For a complete list of seller fees, go to eBay.com Fees.

Once we're satisfied that everything is correct, we officially submit the listing. Since we chose to start the listing immediately, it immediately shows up on the eBay Web site:

Now we have an item for sale on eBay. The area with the blue background only shows up for us. We can make changes to the listing by clicking "Revise your item" as long as no one has placed a bid and there are more than 12 hours left in the auction.

If at least one person places a bid before the auctions ends in seven days, we've got ourselves a buyer. When the auction is over, we'll send our buyer an **invoice** through eBay -- it's basically a one-click process. We click on the "Send Invoice" button either on the auction page or in the sale-confirmation e-mail we receive from eBay, enter any payment details we did not already include in our listing, and hit "Send Invoice."

Once we receive notification from PayPal that the buyer has sent his electronic payment, we'll ship the item to the buyer's confirmed PayPal address and leave positive feedback. Hopefully the buyer will also leave positive feedback once he has received his MP3 player in a timely fashion and finds it to be as we described it in the listing.

Feedback is the best tool available for weeding out the bad sellers and backing up the good ones. Still, with all of the buying and selling that happens on eBay, all of it based on pictures and descriptions, fraud does happen. In the next section, we'll talk about some ways you can protect yourself from common schemes.

Outcome: Second Time's the Charm

On our first attempt, the MP3 player didn't get any bids. But all is not lost. We can **relist** it -- and if it sells the second time, we don't pay any relisting fee (but we do pay the final-value fee). If it doesn't sell, we have to pay the second $0.35 listing fee.

Most likely, the problem is the sheer number of MP3 players listed on eBay -- on October 24, 2005, there are almost 17,000 listings in the "MP3 Players" category, many of them brand-new items in the gigabyte range listed by high-volume sellers at a starting price of $0.99. It's hard to compete with that. Since our player is a low-value item (ancient in consumer electronics terms, refurbished and somewhat of a gamble), it's not cost effective to add any of the fee-based features that might make it stand out, such as bold-face type or gallery status. So we'll give it another shot using some other techniques.

For the second listing, we shortened the title a bit so it's easier to read and dropped the starting price down to $4.99. We made it clearer in the description that its basic functions do definitely work. This time, our item received three bids from two eBay users and sold for $15.50.

Using eBay: Security

The Internet in general is a hotbed of fraud schemes, and eBay is certainly a microcosm of the Internet. Anonymity provides an easy path to cheating people out of money. But while eBay users are anonymous on the surface, eBay almost always knows who they are. In most cases of fraud committed through eBay, the victims do have some recourse.

In order to make buyers feel safer when making purchases on eBay, all tangible items are automatically insured for $200. A recipe that was supposed to be delivered to you via e-mail is not considered a tangible item. But if you purchased a set of speakers that never arrived, and you go through the dispute process and eBay determines you were defrauded, you can get your money back up to $200. As an incentive to use eBay's PayPal payment system, most items purchased through PayPal are covered up to $1,000.

Buyer fraud is typically less damaging than seller fraud. The most common type of fraud a buyer can commit is simply not paying for an item. Sellers can deal with non-paying bidders by filing an Unpaid Item dispute. eBay will then attempt to contact the buyer and get her to pay. If she does not respond to eBay's attempts after eight days, the seller is reimbursed for eBay's cut of the final sale price and can relist the item for free. If the buyer does respond, the dispute can end in one of three ways:

* The buyer decides to pay, and everybody's happy.
* The buyer and the seller decide together to abandon the transaction, the seller gets reimbursed for the final-value fee and relists the item for free, and everybody's happy.
* The seller decides not to deal with the buyer, the buyer gets an unpaid-item strike against her, and the seller gets reimbursed for the final-value fee and relists the item for free.

In the end, the damage to the seller is relatively small. Another type of buyer fraud occurs when a buyer sends false payment. In most cases, this is in the form of a bounced check, and the seller finds out about it before shipping the item. Bounced checks are as common on eBay as they are in the rest of the world, and many sellers choose not to accept personal checks for this reason.

Tips to avoid buyer fraud:

* Always check the feedback of your bidders. If a user has excessive negative feedback, you may be able to cancel the bid.
* If you accept a personal check as payment, never ship the merchandise until the check clears.
* If your buyer doesn't pay, always leave negative feedback so the non-paying bidder has a harder time striking again.

Seller fraud is what what most people think about when they worry about using eBay. There are two main ways in which a buyer can be defrauded by a seller: The item the buyer purchased is dramatically different from how it was described in the listing; or the item simply never arrives.

One thing to keep in mind when you think you've been defrauded is that **miscommunication** is common on eBay. For instance, if you didn't read every word of the auction listing for your item, you may have missed the part the said the seller would be out of town for three weeks and wouldn't be able to ship the item until she returned. This could be why you don't have your item and the seller isn't answering your e-mails. Also, e-mail is not the most straightforward form of communication. If your item hasn't arrived after two weeks, and you've e-mailed the seller but haven't heard back, it's a good idea to check your junk mail folder. Your seller may have sent a response e-mail that just never made it to your inbox. If there's nothing from the seller in your junk folder, you can request that eBay reveal your seller's phone number so you can give him a call and see what's going on.

If you don't get an answer to your phone call (or if your seller lives in another country and it would cost too much money to call), your next step is to start the dispute process. When a buyer believes he has been defrauded, he can file a complaint, and eBay will work to solve the problem. (If you used PayPal, you should file a complaint there first, because your item is probably covered under PayPal's buyer protection policy and there's a separate system for that.) When you file a complaint in eBay's "Item Not Received or Significantly Not as Described" system, eBay will act as middle man between you and your seller to try to settle the dispute. If that fails, you can file a claim to get reimbursed for your purchase (but if you made your purchase using a credit card, you need to file a claim with your credit card company first -- eBay won't reimburse you if your credit card company is willing to).

Tips to avoid seller fraud:

- Always check seller feedback before placing a bid.
- Ask all relevant questions before bidding on an auction. Some sellers think that if they don't say what condition the item is in, it's the buyer's fault if he bids on the item assuming it's in good condition and it turns out to be a piece of junk.
- Always leave negative feedback for unscrupulous sellers -- this makes it harder for them to continue committing fraud.

Fake escrow services are another way in which both buyers and sellers can be defrauded. See eBay Help: Using Escrow to learn about the safest way to use escrow for expensive purchases.

These are the main methods of fraud committed through eBay, but there's another kind of eBay-related fraud that happens outside the eBay Web site. If you receive an e-mail from eBay asking you to update your account information, it's a good idea to be suspicious. **Identity theft** resulting from **spoof e-mails** that look like they're from eBay is a big problem. Many people know this scam as "phishing." These e-mails typically tell you that there is a problem with your credit card number stored on eBay, and unless you update your account information you won't be able to use the site. Sometimes there's an account information form in the e-mail itself, and sometimes there's a link that directs you to what looks like eBay's account information page but in fact is a spoof Web site. When you submit your account information, the scammer gets his hands on your credit card information and your eBay password. (PayPal spoofing is just as common as eBay spoofing, so you should be on the lookout for those e-mails, too. See PayPal: Protect Yourself from Fraudulent Emails to learn more.)

If you're aware of the problem, it's actually pretty easy to avoid getting scammed in this way. First, e-mails from eBay never include account information forms; second, even though the link in the e-mail looks like an eBay URL, once you click on it, you can see in your browser's address bar that you're not at eBay at all. One fairly surefire way to avoid this type of scheme is by downloading the eBay security toolbar, which will simply tell you when you're at a fake site. For a full list of ways to determine a spoof, see eBay: Spoof Email Tutorial.

If you find yourself the victim of one of these scams, and you've submitted your account information in a non-eBay form, you should immediately cancel the credit card number you provided and change your eBay password. In addition to using your credit card, these spoofers can use your eBay identity to cheat people, ruining your eBay reputation in the process.

It's worth noting that you can also become the victim of identity theft simply by providing your credit card number in a seller's own checkout process. Most sellers who have their own checkout process are high-volume sellers with plenty of positive feedback (in the thousands). If you come across a seller with a low feedback number, be wary of providing your credit card information outside the eBay checkout system.

Tips to avoid identity theft:

- Know what a spoof looks like, and always check for the signs before providing any information.
- Always report spoof e-mails to eBay (see What to do about spoofs). eBay will confirm that it's a spoof and investigate the incident.
- Carefully check seller feedback before providing your credit card information in a seller's private checkout form.
  If you're diligent and careful, eBay can be a safe place to shop. Millions of people buy and sell on eBay with no problems at all, and as a result, eBay is thriving. In the next section, we'll take a look at the business of eBay, find out how it began and see what competition is out there.

The Business of eBay

In 1995, computer programmer **Pierre Omidyar** set up a Web site called AuctionWeb as a place for people to auction off their collectibles. The story goes that his girlfriend needed a place to sell her Pez collection, and thus eBay was born. A little bit closer to the truth is that Omidyar, like every other innovative thinker in the computer industry in the early '90s, saw the potential of the Internet and was determined to utilize it. His girlfriend's trouble finding collectors who were interested in buying her Pez collection helped reveal the bid idea that would eventually become eBay. Omidyar advertised AuctionWeb primarily through postings in Usenet groups. Some of the first items on AuctionWeb included a pair of underwear autographed by Marky Mark, a Superman lunchbox circa 1967, an old Sun-1 workstation, a 35,000-square-foot warehouse in Idaho and Omidyar's own broken laser printer (which sold for $14). In 1996, AuctionWeb became eBay.

In 2004, eBay hosted 1.4 billion listings with a total of $34.2 billion changing hands. In September 2005, eBay purchased Skype, a global VoIP service with 54 million customers, for $2.6 billion. It also owns PayPal.com, Half.com, Shopping.com, Kijiji.com, ProStores.com and Rent.com, and it has a 25 percent stake in CraigsList.com. By all financial measures, business in eBay world is good.

eBay Growth		
	Nov. - Dec. 2004	**Jan. - Mar. 2005**
Consolidated Net Revenue	$935.8 million	$1.032 billion
Gross Profit	$759.4 million	$845.4 million
Number of Listings	404.6 million	431.8 million
Gross Merchandise Volume	$9.8 billion	$10.6 billion
Confirmed Registered Users	135.5 million	147.1 million
Source: eBay earning reports, Q4-04 and Q1-05		

The rise of **eBay stores**, where sellers can create their own store fronts and sell items just like they had their own Web site -- except that they pay eBay for each listing and a cut of every sale -- is bringing eBay into the mainstream consumer market and giving people a new revenue stream. A 2005 survey found that approximately 725,000 people living in the United States earned all or part of their income from eBay sales, and another 1.5 million regularly use eBay to earn a little extra cash. The eBay juggernaut has spawned an entire industry that revolves around its platform. Software developers are creating applications to help people find misspelled listings on eBay so they can win items for less than they're worth. Other **auction-related software** includes "sniper" programs that automatically place a user's bid at the last possible second and programs that alert users to outbids and soon-ending auctions on their cell phone or PDA. Brick-and-mortar **eBay consignment shops** exist solely to sell people's unwanted items on eBay if they don't feel like doing it themselves.

EBay isn't the only online auction Web site, but it's by far the biggest. Yahoo!, Amazon and Overstock all have their own auction services, and others include uBid.com, AuctionFire.com and PoliceAuctions.com (where you can bid on government-seized property). There are also dozens of fledgling auction sites that offer free listing and other incentives to draw customers from eBay, but eBay continues to break records. Some people think eBay's success will ultimately lead to legal problems. With almost 5 million new listings per day, it's impossible for eBay to make sure none of them breaks a law. In 1999, eBay cancelled an auction for a human kidney (which had reached a bid price of $5.7 million) and several auctions for large firearms, including a rocket launcher and a bazooka. That year, eBay had 6 million registered users. Now it has 150 million. Although eBay prohibits the sale of human body parts and firearms, it's unclear what type of legal responsibility the company might have if one of those auctions were successfully completed. As of October 2005, eBay is looking at possible fines resulting from the alleged sale of prescription contact lenses on the site, even though "Prescription Drugs and Devices" are on eBay's list of prohibited items.

Its astonishing reach may ultimately be its downfall, but for now, eBay remains the poster child for Internet success.

PayPal

A road map and history

eBook

The idea behind PayPal is simple: Use encryption software to allow people to make financial transfers between computers. That simple idea has turned into one of the world's primary methods of online payment. Despite its occasionally troubled history, including fraud, lawsuits and zealous government regulators, PayPal now boasts over 100 million active accounts in 190 markets worldwide

PayPal is an online payment service that allows individuals and businesses to transfer funds electronically. Here are some of the things you might use PayPal for:

- Send or receive payments for online auctions at eBay and other Web sites
- Purchase or sell goods and services
- Make or receive donations
- Exchange cash with someone

You can send funds to anyone with an e-mail address, whether or not they have a PayPal account. To receive the funds, though, the recipient must have a PayPal account associated with that e-mail address.

Basic PayPal accounts are free, and many financial transactions are free as well, including all purchases from merchants that accept payments using PayPal.

If you have a PayPal account, you can add and withdraw funds in many different ways. You can associate your account with bank accounts or credit cards for more direct transactions, including adding and withdrawing money. Other withdrawal options include using a PayPal debit card to make purchases or get cash from an ATM, or requesting a check in the mail.

In this ebook, we'll show you how to use PayPal, find out how the transactions are made, and learn something about the company's history. Let's start with how to sign up for your own PayPal account.

Signing Up for PayPal

Signing up for PayPal is quick, and doesn't even require you to enter any bank account information. However, if you want to use many of PayPal's features, you'll need to add and verify a checking account or credit card. To get started, just click the "sign up" link at the top of the site's home page.

At the next page, you'll choose whether you want a personal, business or premier account. If you just plan to use PayPal for the occasional eBay auction or online purchase, a personal account is the right choice. If you intend to use PayPal to accept payments for a business, then a business or premier account would be more suitable. If you select a personal account, you can upgrade in the future.

From there, PayPal asks for some basic personal information: your legal first and last name, address, telephone number and e-mail address. You'll also need to check the box indicating that you agree to PayPal's user agreement, privacy policy, acceptable use policy and electronic communications policy. Once you click to create your account, you'll receive an e-mail with instructions for verifying your account and confirming your address.

From here, you should know what PayPal means when it refers to this verification and confirmation process. Having your information vetted by PayPal shows both buyers and sellers that you are less likely to be a scammer.

- A PayPal account is verified if you've associated that account with a current bank account or credit card. This is more than just entering account information. PayPal will ask you to follow certain steps to complete the verification process. For a checking account, for example, PayPal will make two micropayments to that account, usually about five cents each. Then, you'll need to enter the amounts of those micropayments as verification.

- A PayPal account is confirmed if you've completed one of three options to signal to PayPal that the address on your account is valid. The fastest of these is to verify a bank account or credit card matching the address you've entered as the PayPal account's address. As an alternative, you can request a confirmation code by mail after you've had the account for 90 or more days, or you can apply for a PayPal Extras MasterCard which confirms your address by running a credit check.

In the next section, we'll examine what parts make up the PayPal Web site and service.

PayPal Infrastructure

From a buyer's perspective, PayPal changed the way people exchange money online. Behind the scenes, though, it didn't fundamentally change the way merchants interact with banks and credit card companies. PayPal just acts as a middleman.

To understand what that means, consider that credit and debit card transactions travel on several different networks. When a merchant accepts a charge from a card, that merchant pays an interchange, which is a fee of about 10 cents, plus approximately 2 percent of the transaction amount. The interchange is made up of a variety of smaller fees paid to all the different companies that have a part in the transaction: the merchant's bank, the credit card association and the company that issued the card. If someone pays by check, a different network is used, one that costs the merchant less but moves more slowly.

What part does PayPal play in all this? Both buyer and seller deal with PayPal instead of each other. Both sides have provided their bank account or credit card information to PayPal. PayPal, in turn, handles all the transactions with various banks and credit card companies, and pays the interchange.

PayPal makes its own money in two ways. The first is the fees they charge to a payment's recipients. Though most transactions are free for the average user, merchants pay a fee on transactions. PayPal also collects interest on money left in PayPal accounts. All the money held in PayPal accounts is placed into one or more interest-earning bank accounts. An account holders doesn't receive any of the interest gained on the money while it sits in a PayPal account.

PayPal touts its presence as an extra layer as a security feature. That's because everyone's information, including credit card numbers, bank account numbers and address, stays within PayPal. With other online transactions, that information is transmitted across all the networks involved in the transaction, from the buyer to the merchant to the credit card processor.

As an added layer of security, PayPal also offers a PayPal Security Key, which is a portable device that creates a six-digit code every 30 seconds. The user links this key to his or her eBay or PayPal account. The six-digit code is used in conjunction with the user ID and password to create a unique security code. This extra service requires either a one-time purchase of $29.95 for the device or a mobile phone with text messaging to receive codes from a virtual key (the mobile service's SMS charges apply).

Next, let's roll back the clock and see how PayPal came to be the biggest name in online payment services.

PayPal History

Peter Thiel and Max Levchin founded PayPal in December 1998 under the name Confinity. Operating out of Silicon Valley, the idealistic vision of the company was one of a borderless currency, free from governmental controls. When venture capital funding combined with eBay transaction partnerships, PayPal quickly shot up to 1 million users after just 15 months.

However, PayPal's success quickly drew the attention of hackers, scam artists and organized crime groups, who used the service for frauds and money laundering. New security measures stemmed the tide of fraud and customer complaints, but government officials soon stepped in. Regulators and attorneys general in several states, including New York and California, fined PayPal for violations and investigated the company's business practices. Some states, such as Louisiana, banned PayPal from operating in their states altogether. PayPal has since received licenses that allow them to operate in these places.

Despite the initial turmoil, PayPal's market share continued to grow. Initially, PayPal offered new users $10 to join, plus bonuses for referring friends. The service grew so quickly that it soon became the default online payment service. Buyers wanted to use it since so many merchants accepted it, and merchants accepted it because so many buyers were using it.

In February 2002, PayPal held its IPO, opening at $15.41 per share and closing the day's trading above the $20 mark. PayPal owes much of its initial growth to eBay users who promoted PayPal as a way to exchange money for their online auctions. PayPal even beat eBay at the online payment business, trumping eBay's in-house payment system Billpoint so thoroughly that in October 2002, eBay bought PayPal for $1.4 billion in stock. eBay phased out Billpoint and integrated PayPal into its services. Sellers with PayPal accounts can place icons in their auctions so that buyers can simply click on the PayPal logo when they win an auction to make an immediate payment.

Since 2002, PayPal has remained a steady leader in providing online transaction services. It expanded its services in the United States to include such features as debit cards for the account. By the end of 2011, PayPal was available in over 100 markets for transactions in 25 international currencies. This worldwide expansion has brought PayPal a little closer to that original idealistic vision from Thiel and Levchin.

In the next section, we'll learn about the different types of PayPal accounts.

PayPal Account Types

Earlier, we discovered that PayPal has three account types: Personal, Premier and Business. All these account types can use the following core PayPal functions:

- Sending money
- Requesting money
- Using auction tools
- Making payments from a Web site
- Debit card services
- Customer service

Besides these functions, the three accounts also share certain features and limitations. For example, if you have a verified account, you can send up to $10,000 in a single transaction, and there are generally no transaction fees for sending and receiving money between PayPal accounts. However, you'll pay a fee when using a PayPal debit card or receiving money for something that requires a currency exchange. Unverified accounts, including those without an associated bank account or credit card, have more restrictive sending and withdraw limits. You can determine the limits on your account by clicking a "view limits" link near the top of the page after you sign in to PayPal [source: PayPal].

The three PayPal account types differ in some important ways. First, Personal accounts give you access to the core features, but that's all. PayPal handles customer support for Personal accounts primarily by e-mail or through a virtual customer support agent at the PayPal Web site. There's a phone number available, but it's not toll-free and may have extensive wait times.

Premier and Business accounts are almost the same. The main difference is that a Business account must be registered with a business or group name, while a Premier account can be registered with a business, group or individual. Also, you can set up multiple users to access a business account.

In addition to PayPal's core functions, Business and Premier accounts provide these options:

- Accepting debit and credit card payments
- Allowing senders to set up recurring payments (subscriptions)
- Unlimited use of a PayPal ATM/debit card

Business and Premier Accounts also get a toll-free customer service number and extended customer service hours. These extra features come at the cost of transaction fees, which we'll take a closer look at later.

If you're starting your own PayPal account for a business, compare the fees and services from PayPal against other credit card transaction services to determine which works best for your needs. Consider that with PayPal, most of the code you'll need to add to a Web site is automated for you, too. Shopping cart functions or "pay now" buttons may not be as easy to implement through other services.

Once you have your account, you're ready to send and receive money. Next, let's look at how to use PayPal for sending money.

Using PayPal: Sending Funds

Though PayPal rose to stardom via eBay, one of the keys to PayPal's success has been its ability to expand beyond that market. You can use it to send money to a friend, donate to charity and buy items online. In order to send money using your PayPal account, you'll need one of two things:

Funds already transferred to your PayPal account before the transaction

An instant transfer account, usually a checking or savings account, from which PayPal will withdraw the necessary funds to cover the transaction

From there, it's just a matter of knowing your recipient. To send money to a person, all you need is the e-mail address associated with that person's PayPal account. For an organization or business, you can usually send money from a PayPal link at its Web site.

From the sender's perspective, PayPal is a free service. In fact, if you send money directly from a checking or savings account, there are never any fees involved. The one exception would be if you pay for something by taking a cash advance from your credit card. While PayPal might not charge you for this service, your credit card provider probably will.

One thing to be aware of when sending money, particularly with donations, is designating the money's purpose. In some cases, you'll link from the recipient's Web site to a shopping cart page that automatically makes this selection for you. If you click to "Send Money" from the PayPal Web site, you have the following two tabs of options to indicate whether you're buying something or just sending money:

Purchase tab with the options of Goods, Services or eBay items

Personal tab with the options of Gift, Payment owed, Cash advance, Living expense, Other

After you send money, the record of your transaction should appear on the History page at PayPal.com. If necessary, you can search that history for a specific time in the past. If you click the "details" link for a transaction, you can view all the details, including the amount, date, recipient and a unique transaction ID used by PayPal to track your transaction. If you ever dispute a transaction, customer service will use this transaction number when handling the dispute from both sides, sender and recipient.

If a Web site only accepts credit cards and not PayPal, you can still use funds in your PayPal account to make a purchase. To do this, you'll need to request a PayPal debit card which operates on the Master Card network. You can use that card number with any merchant who accepts MasterCard, and the funds will be deducted from the PayPal account. This service is free, but has a daily spending limit of $3,000. That debit card can also be used at ATMs to withdraw up to $400 in cash daily from your PayPal account, and it can earn 1 percent cash back on purchases if you're enrolled for PayPal Preferred Rewards through eBay.

In the next section, we'll see how both personal users and merchants can use PayPal to accept payments.

Using PayPal: Receiving Funds

If you want to use PayPal to receive money, you have a range of options available. If you give someone the e-mail address associated with your PayPal account, that person can send you money from their own PayPal account. If you're selling items on eBay, you can select PayPal as an option for accepting payment through eBay. If you're selling from your own store or Web site, there are a number of options available for completing sales transactions with PayPal, including the following:

- Adding a PayPal "buy now" button for each item you want to sell
- Integrating a PayPal shopping cart with your Web site using the PayPal application programming interface (API)
- Accepting payments offline or off-site to process later using PayPal's Virtual Terminal

When you're signed in to PayPal, click the "merchant services" tab to see all the options available to you as a seller. Cost and availability of these services depend on which Web site payments type you've selected for your account. You'll have the "standard" type by default as a recipient, but you can upgrade to the "pro" type for a $30 monthly subscription fee. Merchants with a moderate to high volume of transactions each month should choose the pro type to avoid some of the fees commonly charged by other payment processing services, such as gateway and downgrade fees.

From the merchant services page, you can select the wizard tools to set up new "buy now" or "add to cart" buttons for your site. This generates code you can simply copy and paste into the HTML for your Web pages. When a buyer clicks one of these buttons, your site links to a shopping cart at PayPal's site to complete the transaction. This takes the burden off you, as a seller, of managing how that online shopping cart and checkout should look and function.

For more extensive integration, including hosting a PayPal-powered shopping cart from your own site, you'll need to use the PayPal API. If you're not savvy with computer programming or Web site development, this is a task you'll want to delegate to someone who is.

Once you're set up to receive money, the burden is on you as the recipient to cover the transaction costs. PayPal charges its business and premier account holders a per-transaction cost of 30 cents, plus 2.9 percent of the transaction amount. If the merchant has a higher sales volume within a month, that percentage could drop to as low as 1.9 percent. PayPal also charges fees for exchanging between its 25 accepted currencies in international transactions. All these fees help cover PayPal's customer support and other services reserved for business and premier customers.

The last option shown above is accepting offline and off-site payments. This means you've taken the buyer's name and credit card information outside of PayPal. You can enter that information and process the transaction using PayPal's virtual terminal service. This tool is available from the merchant services page at PayPal.com. Unlike other fee-based services at PayPal, virtual terminal requires a subscription of $30 per month, or the equivalent of upgrading to a Web site payments pro account. The per-transaction costs mentioned above still apply in addition to this fee.

As a recipient, you can remove money from your PayPal account by making a withdrawal. These are your options for making the withdrawal:

- Transfer money to a bank account associated with your PayPal account
- Request that PayPal mail you a paper check for a certain amount
- Make purchases using a PayPal debit card

So far, we've covered how to send and receive money with PayPal and how PayPal accounts work. On the next page, we'll take a closer look at the challenges PayPal has faced and the continued controversy over its business practices.

Problems with PayPal

Though PayPal does have millions of seemingly satisfied customers, not all users have had such a pleasant experience. In fact, so many people have felt slighted by PayPal that entire Web sites exist to discuss problems about PayPal and mock its business practices. The most prominent is PayPal Sucks.

The biggest criticism of PayPal is that it acts like a bank, but it isn't regulated like one. This means that PayPal offers none of the protection that real banks offer, and it isn't required to maintain any of the security, customer service or dispute resolution services that banks provide. At the same time, PayPal holds large amounts of their customers' money, makes millions of financial transactions and even offers credit and debit cards.

So why isn't it considered a bank? In 2002, the Federal Deposit Insurance Corporation (FDIC) declared that because PayPal didn't meet the federal definition of an entity accepting deposits as a bank, hold any physical money or have a bank charter, it was not a bank [source: Wolverton]. In other words, PayPal isn't a bank because it doesn't call itself a bank. As a result, most states license PayPal as a "money service."

One of the most common problems encountered by PayPal users is the sudden and inexplicable freezing of their accounts. If your PayPal account is frozen, you can't add or withdraw any funds from your account, and you're required to go through a long, complicated process to verify your identity. Some users claim that PayPal has simply seized their funds and never returned them. Other complaints against PayPal include rude customer service representatives, a long and confusing User Agreement and loose hiring practices that may have led to account fraud. Despite these criticisms, PayPal continues to be the most popular money transfer service for online transactions